Great Journeys

The Spice Trade

Don Wells

WEIGL PUBLISHERS INC.

Published by Weigl Publishers Inc.
350 5th Avenue, Suite 3304, PMB 6G
New York, NY 10118-0069

Web site: www.weigl.com
Copyright 2005 WEIGL PUBLISHERS INC.
All rights reserved. No part of this publication may be reproduced, stored in a retrieval system, or transmitted in any form or by any means, electronic,mechanical, photocopying, recording, or otherwise, without the prior written permission of the publisher.

All of the Internet URLs given in the book were valid at the time of publication. However, due to the dynamic nature of the Internet, some addresses may have changed, or sites may have ceased to exist since publication. While the author and publisher regret any inconvenience this may cause readers, no responsibility for any such changes can be accepted by either the author or the publisher.

Library of Congress Cataloging-in-Publication Data
Wells, Donald.
  The spice trade / Donald Wells.
     p. cm.
  Includes bibliographical references and index.
  ISBN 1-59036-208-X (library binding : alk. paper) — ISBN 1-59036-261-6 (pbk.)
  1. Spice trade--History. I. Title.
  HD9210.A2W45 2004
  382'.4566453--dc22

2004002878
Printed in the United States of America
1 2 3 4 5 6 7 8 9 0   09 08 07 06 05 04

Project Coordinator
Donald Wells
Substantive Editor
Tina Schwartzenberger
Copy Editor
Heather C. Hudak
Photo Researcher
Andrea Harvey
Design & Layout
Bryan Pezzi

Credits
Every reasonable effort has been made to trace ownership and to obtain permission to reprint copyright material. The publishers would be pleased to have any errors or omissions brought to their attention so that they may be corrected in subsequent printings.

Cover: Spice shop in Taroudannt, Morocco (**Kurt-Michael Westermann/CORBIS/MAGMA; Corel Corporation:** pages 1, 5B, 19, 24; **Bryan Pezzi:** pages 12, 13; **Photos.com:** pages 3, 4, 5T, 6, 7, 8, 10, 11, 14, 15T, 15B 16, 17T, 17B 18, 20, 22, 23T, 23B, 25R, 26; **PhotoSpin Inc.:** page 25L; **Jim Steinhart:** pages 9, 21, 27.

On the Cover: Taroudannt, Morocco, and its marketplace were once important stops for caravans traveling south to trade in spices and ivory.

Contents

The Long History of Spice Use ..4

The Importance of Spices 6

Age of the Sail 8

The Lure of Spices 10

Maps 12

Spice Wars 14

The Influence
of the Spice Trade 16

Legendary People
in the Spice Trade 18

A Sailor's Life 20

Pliny the Elder's
Natural History 22

Modern Spice Trade 24

Lasting Effects 26

Spice Trade Time Line 28

Activity: Making a
Simple Astrolabe 29

Quiz 30

Further Research 30

Glossary 31

Index 32

The Long History of Spice Use

Spices are substances made from plants that give a special flavor to food. In ancient times, spices were used in many ways. Spices were used to season food at Roman feasts. They were used to make medicines. Bay leaves were made into crowns for winners at ancient Greece's Olympic games. The ancient Romans believed bay leaves protected them against thunder and the **plague**. Spice-flavored wines were popular. Spice also was burned as **incense** in temples.

Archeologists believe that by 50,000 BC people had discovered that parts of certain **aromatic** plants improve the taste of food. Egyptian hieroglyphics on the walls of the pyramids and passages in the *Bible* show that spices played an important role in the lives of ancient people. Some of the spices, **herbs**, and seeds used today were grown by the early people of the western world.

Fascinating Fact
The word *aroma* was the ancient Greek word for "spice."

Today, spices are inexpensive. Almost everyone can afford to use black pepper, cinnamon, cloves, or ginger. At one time, these fragrant bits of bark, leaves, and seeds were so expensive that people were willing to risk their lives to obtain them.

Spices such as cumin, sage, and oregano can be found in kitchens across North America.

The Spice Islands

The term *Spice Islands* is most commonly used to refer to small volcanic islands in the Maluku Province of Indonesia. These islands were the original source of cloves, mace, and nutmeg. Portuguese sailors were the first to visit these islands in 1512. However, in the seventeenth century, the Dutch conquered the islands and established control over the clove trade. On two occasions, the British acquired control of the islands from the Dutch. In the early nineteenth century, the Dutch gained and kept control of the islands until World War II, when they became part of Indonesia. Other islands known for their spice production include the Tanzanian Islands of Zanzibar, Mafia Island, and Pemba. These islands are also referred to as the Spice Islands.

More than 17,000 islands make up the country of Indonesia.

Most of the world's spices originated in Southeast Asia.

The Importance of Spices

In ancient times, spices were used for more than flavoring food. Spices came in the form of bark, ointments, powders, herbs, roots, and **resins**. Spices were used in religious rituals to invoke, or call upon, the gods, expel evil spirits, and pay tribute to emperors.

Queen Hatshepsut of Egypt used cinnamon as a perfume as early as 1500 BC. The Romans added cardamom to their henna-flower perfume. They also used cinnamon to prevent moths from eating clothing. Hippocrates, the famous Greek physician, prescribed pepper as a cure for disease. Egyptians used a mixture of spices, including cloves, to help preserve **mummies**. Crateuas, a famous Greek physician, wrote about a mixture of spices that could protect people against poison. This mixture included anise, cardamom, cassia, cumin, and ginger.

Fascinating Fact
Anise tastes like licorice. Anise oil is distilled and used to flavor licorice candy.

In eleventh-century Europe, pepper was more valuable than gold. People often paid their rent in peppercorns. Debts were erased for a payment of pepper. Families included pepper in their daughters' **dowries**. Government officials accepted pepper bribes for favors.

Spices were very important and valuable. Traders risked their lives to obtain them. They created stories to protect the location of spices. Traders even fought wars to gain control over the spice trade routes.

Pepper belongs to the same plant family as potatoes and tomatoes.

Pepper, King of Spices

Pepper, the most common spice in the world, grows on vines. The pepper used today is the dried fruit of the vine. Green pepper comes from unripe fruit that is picked young. Black pepper comes from unripe peppercorns. White pepper comes from fully ripened fruit.

Pepper was first used 4,000 years ago. It was the first spice known to Europeans. India was the original source of pepper. By the fourth century BC, Romans used pepper to flavor food and as medicine. For hundreds of years, Arabian spice traders kept the location of pepper secret. Today, India produces 40 percent of the world's pepper. Half the world's pepper is grown in Brazil and Indonesia. The United States is the world's largest pepper importer, buying nearly 42,500 tons (38,555 metric tonnes) a year.

Some of the most common spices are cinnamon, dill, nutmeg, and bay leaves.

Age of the Sail

During the Middle Ages, Italian and Muslim traders controlled Asian trade goods traveling to Europe. European countries did not want to pay the high prices charged by the Italians and Muslims for silk, spices, and other luxury items shipped from Asia.

The telescope and the compass improved navigation.

By the fifteenth century, technological advances enabled European traders to attempt to find a direct sea route from Europe to Asia. Northern Europeans designed and built larger, faster, and stronger ships. There was a new compass. Navigators could use the astrolabe invented by Arabian sailors to estimate their distance from the **equator**.

To **navigate**, sailors need to know the position where their voyage begins, their location at sea, and their destination. In the fifteenth century, there was no accurate way to measure longitude, which is the distance east or west of Greenwich, an area in the city of London, England. Sailors could not determine the speed at which a ship was traveling. However, fifteenth-century navigators could estimate the time of day or night. They could determine the direction of travel and calculate the latitude, or how far north or south the ship was from the equator. With improvements to ships and navigational aids, fifteenth-century European explorers searched the world's oceans for new routes to Asia.

Fascinating Fact
The Portuguese explorer Vasco da Gama reached India in 1498 and established the first direct sea route from Europe to Asia. He would not have been able to complete this journey without improvements to ships and navigational aids.

Fifteenth-century Maps

Portuguese sailors explored the Atlantic Ocean and the southern coast of Africa during the 1440s. Portuguese mapmakers used information gathered during these expeditions to update maps. By 1502, Portuguese mapmakers were creating master charts with up-to-date information about coastlines and oceans. These master charts were used to create local **nautical** charts. By 1505, each of the major Atlantic ports had a local nautical chart. These charts detailed the depth of the sea, dangers such as ridges of sand, rock, or coral near the ocean's surface, and other information needed to guide sailors safely into port. These maps were often treated as national or commercial secrets.

Many sixteenth-century ships were used for more than 65 years.

The Lure of Spices

As early as 950 BC, Arabian merchants had a **monopoly** in the spice trade. Their only competition was from the **Phoenicians**, who navigated from the Mediterranean Sea around Africa to Asia in the seventh century BC. In the first century AD, the Romans grew tired of paying Arabian merchants high prices for spices. The Romans discovered a sea route that allowed them to trade with India and break the Arabian monopoly. Spice use in Europe declined after the fall of the Roman Empire.

In the seventh century AD, Arabian merchants once again took control of the spice trade between Asia and Europe. The Arabian monopoly made spices expensive in Europe. Merchants from Venice, Italy, distributed the spices once they reached Europe. This system made spices a luxury few people could afford.

Tired of paying Arabian and Venetian merchants' high prices for spices, Spain and Portugal financed dozens of expeditions to find a sea route from Europe to Asia. After Vasco da Gama established a sea route to India in 1498, the Arabian and Venetian monopoly ended. Numerous Portuguese explorers returned to Portugal with loads of spices. As a result of this new spice supply, the price of pepper in Lisbon fell to one-fifth the price charged in Venice.

> **Fascinating Fact**
> The Chinese began buying cloves from India in 100 BC. In ancient times, cloves were among the world's most expensive spices.

Spices are sold in bulk in markets around the world.

The Monsoon Winds

Monsoon winds were important to the ancient sea trade. The term *monsoon* refers to the strong winds and heavy rains that characterize the Asian climate. Monsoon winds blew in opposite directions over the same routes every 6 months. Arabian and Indian sailors used the monsoon winds to travel long distances across the Arabian Sea, the Indian Ocean, and the Bay of Bengal. Arabian and Indian traders controlled the spice market by concealing the true source of spices and the secret of the monsoon winds for centuries. Mediterranean sailors from Egypt and Rome did not know about the monsoon wind patterns until the first century BC. An Indian sailor who survived a shipwreck revealed the secret to Egyptian officials. During the following century, Rome used the knowledge of the monsoon winds to establish direct trade with India.

Goods such as spices are delivered throughout Venice, Italy, by boats that travel on the city's famous canal system.

Maps

Traders in search of a sea route to Asia did not know what to expect. Maps were made after each new expedition to include new information. Eventually, maps were produced that contained detailed information about the types of currents, ports, and winds a trader would encounter on a trip from Europe to Asia.

Indonesia and the Spice Islands

Spice Trade Routes AD 1600s

Spice Wars

From the fifteenth to eighteenth centuries, Great Britain, Holland, Portugal, and Spain fought wars in order to gain control of the spice trade. The Portuguese controlled the spice trade during the sixteenth century. They established bases at Goa on the west coast of India and Malacca on the west coast of the country now known as Malaysia. The Portuguese controlled the sea routes in the Indian Ocean and between the Indian Ocean and China.

The Dutch were the biggest threat to Portugal's monopoly of the spice trade. In the 1590s, Dutch merchants became rich and powerful by transporting other people's goods along trade routes in the Mediterranean Sea, Atlantic Ocean, and Indian Ocean. By 1641, Dutch armies were powerful and able to conquer Malacca. In 1650, they gained control of the cinnamon trade in Sri Lanka. In 1663, they controlled the best pepper ports in India. Before the end of the seventeenth century, the Dutch were in complete control of the spice trade.

By 1796, the British had captured Malacca and most of the Spice Islands controlled by Holland. This ended Holland's monopoly of the spice trade. In the early 1800s, spice plants were smuggled to other parts of the world. The spice trade was no longer confined to Asia.

Ginger is used as medicine in China and India. It is often used to cure the common cold.

Dutch East India Company

In 1602, an association of merchants formed the Dutch East India Company. The company established the first European settlement in South Africa on the Cape of Good Hope in 1652. At the peak of its power in 1669, the company had 40 warships, 150 merchant ships, and 10,000 soldiers. By 1670, it was the richest company in the world. In the eighteenth century, internal conflicts, the growth of British and French power, and the consequences of a harsh policy toward the **indigenous** people under its control caused the decline of the company. By 1798, the company was bankrupt. The Dutch government took over its possessions and debts.

When the first Dutch ship arrived from India with a cargo of spices in 1600, Amsterdam immediately became Europe's new center for the spice trade.

Fascinating Fact
When spice prices fell, Dutch merchants burned cinnamon and clove trees to keep prices high. They soaked nutmeg in "milk of lime," a solution they thought would stop the seeds from growing and prevent rivals from producing their own trees.

The Influence of the Spice Trade

The spice trade was responsible for two important events in history. The first event was the spread of Islam throughout the Middle East, Asia, and Southeast Asia. Islam is a religion in which followers believe a man named Mohammed was the last prophet of God. The second event was the European Age of Exploration in the fifteenth and sixteenth centuries.

Spice trading was important to the Islamic religion. The prophet Mohammed married a woman from a spice-trading family. Islamic spice traders spread their religion along trade routes as far as Indonesia and the Philippines. Without the spice trade, Islam would not have become a major religion outside of the Arab world.

During the fifteenth century, Islamic merchants controlled the spice trade. The trade routes they used were largely on land. Local rulers charged taxes for spices shipped through their territory. Taxes made spices expensive. The high prices caused European explorers to search for a sea route to the Spice Islands. The fifteenth- and sixteenth-century European expeditions became known as the Age of Exploration.

The Age of Exploration changed the world. It resulted in a vast exchange of people, plants, animals, ideas, and technology. There were many positive effects of the Age of Exploration, such as the exchange of foods between Europe and the Americas. There were also negative effects, such as the exchange of diseases.

Spices are often traded for other goods or sold in street markets in countries such as India.

Spread of Islam

Before Islam monopolized the spice trade, merchants did not travel the entire length of a trade route. Trade was indirect and resembled a chain. Spices were traded from one group of merchants to another. No single group made the entire journey. When Islamic forces gained control over the spice trade, Arabian merchants traveled the entire length of the trade routes. They did not rely on others to deliver the spices. Arab traders spread their religion as they traveled.

Muslims are the followers of the prophet Mohammed. They pray five times every day.

Fascinating Fact
When Christopher Columbus reached the Caribbean Islands, he thought he had sailed all the way to Asia. He died without knowing he had not reached Asia.

Legendary People in the Spice Trade

The Prophet Mohammed

Mohammed was born in the Arab trading city of Mecca in about AD 570. His parents died when he was young. At 25 years of age, Mohammed married a widow named Khadija who owned a **caravan** company.

During one trading journey when he was about 40 years of age, Mohammed encountered the angel Gabriel. The angel Gabriel told him he was to become the messenger of God. Following his prophetic experience, Mohammed began spreading the teachings he learned and developed a code of behavior he said was the word of Allah, or God. This code of behavior is known as the *Quran*, or *Koran*.

The people who accepted Mohammed's teachings came to be known as Muslims. Their religion is *Islam*, an Arabic word that means "surrender."

Mohammed died in 632 and left his followers to carry on the traditions he had begun. During the two centuries after Mohammed's death, the laws of Islam were collected. They are called the *Shariah*.

By the eighth-century AD, Muslims controlled the Atlantic coast of Spain, North Africa, Arabia, Iran, India, and the spice islands of what is now known as Indonesia.

Queen of Sheba

The Queen of Sheba is a legendary figure said to have ruled over a kingdom in Yemen on the Arabian Peninsula. While many women are mentioned in the *Bible* and the *Koran*, the Queen of Sheba is the only woman documented in both books. According to the biblical account, the Queen of Sheba traveled to Israel at the head of a caravan carrying, among other things, spices. The queen had heard about the wisdom of King Solomon, the ruler of Israel. She wanted to test him. Some people believe these events took place around 960 BC and that Sheba was trying to forge a trade link with Israel. Historians date the beginning of the Arabian monopoly of the spice trade to this time. Until recently, many biblical scholars believed the episode between the Queen of Sheba and King Solomon was a fictional, romantic tale. However, some historical evidence suggests that the Queen of Sheba was a real person. Also, archeological discoveries in Yemen show that a rich, spice-trading kingdom existed during the tenth century BC. Biblical stories such as the King Solomon and Queen of Sheba romance and the three wise men bringing spices to the baby Jesus show that spices were considered gifts fit for kings in ancient times.

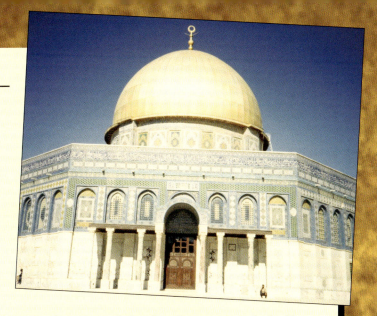

The Dome of the Rock mosque is built on the site of King Solomon's temple in Jerusalem. The site is sacred to both Jewish and Muslim people.

A Sailor's Life

Life on fifteenth- and sixteenth-century European ships was difficult. Sailors were isolated from life on shore for months and sometimes years. They lived in cramped conditions. They slept on the ship's deck. They were exposed to disease. They had to endure poor food and pay. Above all, sailors faced daily dangers from the sea and weather.

Food on European ships included salt beef or pork, cheese, fish, some form of ship's biscuit, and a beverage similar to beer called ale. The quality of the food was often poor because of improper storage, lack of ventilation, and poor drainage. Rats and insects on the ship ate and damaged food. Biscuits were often filled with maggots and **weevils**. Many ships' suppliers were dishonest and sent rotten food as supplies for ships. The ship's cook was often a sailor who was wounded and unfit for other duties. Food was cooked on the open deck.

Fascinating Fact
Sea-shanties were work songs sung on ships. These songs helped sailors perform repetitive tasks such as hauling on ropes.

As well as the cook, a ship's crew usually included a parson, or minister, a surgeon, a master gunner, a boatswain who was in charge of the sails, a carpenter, and a quartermaster who helped the captain with navigation and other duties. Other crew members carried out jobs such as keeping watch for danger or land, handling sails, and cleaning decks.

Many sailors believed that having a cat on board a ship would bring good luck.

Disease and Accidents on the High Seas

There was a great deal of illness at sea. Sailors were often cold and wet. Rats carried disease. The poor diet caused **malnutrition** and illnesses such as **scurvy**. In the late sixteenth century, Sir Richard Hawkins discovered that a daily dose of orange or lemon juice could prevent scurvy. Without the vitamin C contained in these juices, scurvy could rot the skin and gums and cause teeth to fall out.

Sailors also suffered accidents. They risked death or injury in times of battle. Ships' surgeons worked in cramped and unsanitary conditions. There was no **anaesthetic** for patients having amputations. Infection and gangrene, or the rotting of flesh, were common.

Sixteenth-century sailors often tied themselves down to avoid being thrown overboard while they slept on the ship's deck.

Pliny the Elder's Natural History

The following passage from *Natural History* was written by Pliny the Elder (AD 23–79). Pliny the Elder was a Roman soldier and government official. His book *Natural History* is an encyclopedia that contains more than 20,000 "facts" about the ancient world from more than 2,000 earlier texts. This book includes information about subjects from astronomy to zoology. *Natural History* is one of the most important sources of ancient knowledge and beliefs. In the following excerpt, Pliny points out that Arab traders have been misleading Roman customers about the dangers involved in the spice trade.

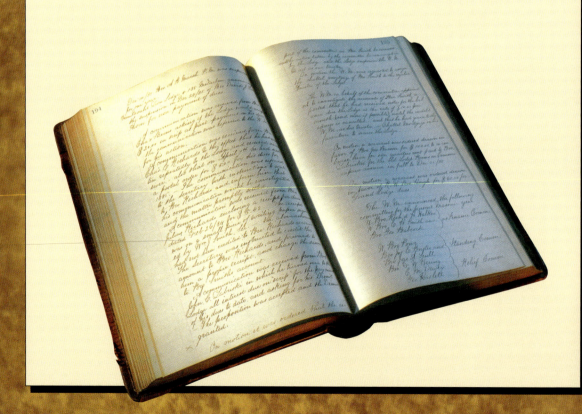

Old tales were invented by the Arabians to raise the price of their goods. There is an accompanying story that under the reflected rays of the sun at midday an indescribable sort of collective odor is given off from the whole of the peninsula, which is due to the harmoniously blended exhalation of all those aromas, and that the first news of Arabia received by the fleets of Alexander the Great were these odors, wafted far out to sea. All these stories are nonsense. In fact cinnamomum, which is the same thing as cinnamum, grows in "Ethiopia," which is linked by intermarriage with the Cave dwellers. These buy it from their neighbors and bring it over vast seas on rafts which have no rudders to steer them, no oars to push them, no sails to propel them, indeed no motive power at all but man alone and his courage. What is more, they take to sea in winter, around the solstice, which is when the east winds blow their hardest. These winds drive them on the proper course across the bays. When they have rounded the Cape, a west-north-west wind will land them in the harbor called Ocilia, so that is the trading place they prefer. They say that their traders take almost five years there and back, and that many die. On the return journey they take glassware and bronze ware, clothing, brooches, bracelets and necklaces.

Cinnamon comes from the inner bark of a tropical evergreen tree. It is sold ground or in sticks of the dried bark.

Modern Spice Trade

Most of the spices that once ruled the spice trade, including cinnamon, cloves, ginger, nutmeg, and pepper, are still grown in Asia. However, many spices, herbs, and aromatic seeds are now grown in the Western Hemisphere. Brazil is a major supplier of pepper. The Caribbean island Grenada grows nutmeg. Jamaica grows ginger and allspice. El Salvador, Nicaragua, and the United States grow sesame seed. The U.S. state of California grows basil, capsicum peppers, mint, paprika, parsley, sage, tarragon, and mustard, dill, and fennel seeds.

Fascinating Fact
Cloves can be used as air fresheners and to repel moths.

Today, the United States is the largest spice importer. New York City is the center of the spice trade. Imported spices enter the U.S. through ports on both coasts, but the largest amount comes through New York City. Spices usually arrive in an unprocessed form. They are inspected for cleanliness and must pass U.S. Food and Drug Administration and American Spice Trade Association standards before they clear the port. After they pass inspection, spices are sent to spice-grinding plants where they are inspected, cleaned, processed, and packaged. Today, the spice industry also offers extracts of spices in which the essences are concentrated from the raw products.

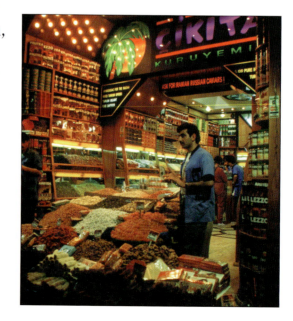

The Misir Carsisi, or Spice Bazaar, is the center of the spice trade in Istanbul, Turkey.

Shipping Spices

Today, spices are harvested and shipped to spice facilities using the same methods used by ancient spice farmers and traders. Spices are picked by hand, **dehydrated**, placed in burlap bags, and shipped to their destinations in a whole, natural, dried state. Most spice dehydration takes place in the field. In the spice trade, this is known as Sun drying. Other spices are air dried in hot-air drying tunnels. Drying reduces the moisture content in spices. Less moisture means spices weigh less and cost less to ship.

In 1983, the United States imported a record 385 million pounds (175 million kilograms) of spices, herbs, and aromatic seeds. Most of these spices arrived in New York City.

Lasting Effects

Without the spice trade, Islam would not have become a common religion outside of the Arab world. Muslim merchants who engaged in the spice trade spread the word about their religion. Muslim traders hoped their interaction with people along trade routes would attract converts to Islam.

The spice traders' strategy was successful. Today, Islam is one of the most prominent religions in the world. It is practiced in places such as China, Indonesia, Russia, Saudi Arabia, Spain, and Syria.

> **Fascinating Fact**
> Today, chemists can make spice essences and flavors from inexpensive, abundant raw materials. Vanilla can be made from wood pulp and coal tar.

The European Age of Exploration was fueled by the search for sea routes that led to the source of spices. It had a lasting impact on Asia, Africa, Europe, and the Americas. European nations competed for colonies across the globe. These colonies were exploited for their raw materials, such as spices, and used as new markets for European goods. Europeans had little regard for most of the indigenous people who lived in these areas. As a result, there was great loss of life and culture. Also, because of the need for a reliable labor source, slaves were transported from Africa to the Americas in large numbers. The Age of Exploration was a turning point in history because it changed the way people lived.

Scientists have found that the spice oregano may help prevent cancer.

The Spice Heist

The French stole cinnamon, clove, and nutmeg plants from the Dutch-controlled Spice Islands in the late seventeenth century. This marked the beginning of the end of spice monopolies. After the theft of these plants, spice cultivation spread to other tropical areas such as the Caribbean Islands and South America. The first "spice heist" was achieved by Pierre Poivre. He learned about spices when he was captured by the British on his way home from China. Once he was released by the British, he joined the French East India Company and stole spice plants from the Dutch. He planted these spice plants on the East African islands of Mauritius and Reunion, which were then under French control.

Pepper is grown in many places. The best pepper is still grown in the Kerala region located on the southwestern tip of India.

Spice Trade Time Line

50,000 BC
People begin using certain leaves to improve the taste of meat.

1453 BC
The Greeks begin the Olympic Games, and victors are awarded bay leaf wreaths.

AD 595
Mohammed weds a wealthy widow involved in the spice trade. His followers combine missionary work with spice trading in the East and build a spice monopoly.

900
Venice, Italy, becomes the spice center of Europe.

1418
Prince Henry the Navigator of Portugal establishes a navigation college.

1492
Christopher Columbus sets sail in search of a more direct route to Asia's spice riches.

1498
Vasco da Gama reaches Calicut, India, a major Asian spice center. As a result of direct trade between Portugal and India, pepper prices fall in Europe.

1585
A West Indies ship arrives in Europe with a cargo of Jamaican ginger, the first oriental spice to be grown successfully in the New World.

1600
The British East India Company is founded.

1602
The Dutch East India Company is founded.

1672
Elihu Yale reaches India and starts a spice business. He becomes rich and uses his money to found Yale University.

1821
The first U.S. spice-grinding company starts in Boston, Massachusetts.

1907
The American Spice Trade Association is formed.

1969
Spices reach the Moon as seasoning in the Apollo astronaut's food.

Activity: Making a Simple Astrolabe

What you need to make a simple astrolabe:

- string
- protractor
- tape measure
- drinking straw
- washer or other weight
- clear tape

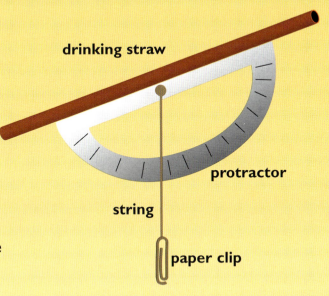

Procedure:

1. Lay the protractor on a flat surface with the numbered side up. Find the hole in the middle of the protractor's base (straight side).

2. Thread the string through the hole and through the weight. Tie the string into a loop. If there is no hole, thread the weight onto the string and tie it into a loop. Tape the loop to the middle of the base.

3. Place the straw on top of the protractor so that one end of the straw crosses the middle of the base and the other end lays along the 90° mark. Leave about 1 inch (2.5 centimeters) of the straw below the base of the protractor and most of the straw above the protractor.

4. Tape the straw firmly into place.

5. Lay the straw along the edge of a desk or table so that the straw is horizontal and the string hangs down vertically. Make sure that the string hangs along the 0° line on the protractor when the straw is horizontal. Make adjustments if necessary. It is important to make sure the string can swing freely.

To use the astrolabe, look at the top of an object through the straw. Have someone read the altitude in degrees from the side of the astrolabe. The point where the string crosses the scale is the proper measurement.

29

1. When do archeologists believe people discovered that some plants improved the taste of food?

2. Does pepper grow on trees?

3. Which city controlled the European spice trade in the Middle Ages?

4. Which Portuguese explorer reached India by sea in 1498?

5. When was the Dutch East India Company formed?

6. Name one reason for the European Age of Exploration.

7. What causes scurvy?

8. How many "facts" are contained in Pliny the Elder's book *Natural History*?

9. Which country is the largest importer of spices today?

10. Which religion spread beyond its birthplace as a result of the spice trade?

Answers on page 32.

Web sites
www.learner.org/exhibits/ renaissance/spicetrade
An interactive lesson where students play the role of a Renaissance ship owner who trades goods around the world. Students need to make decisions about how to prepare for their "journeys," including which routes to take, how to finance their voyages, and more.

academic.emporia.edu/aberjame/ map/h_map/h_map.htm
This Web site contains a brief history of maps.

www.thehistorychannel.com
This Web site contains information about explorers, Spice Islands, and much more.

Books
Milton, Giles. *Nathaniel's Nutmeg*. New York: Farrar, Straus and Giroux, 1999.

Torrey, Michele. *To the Edge of the World*. New York: Alfred A. Knopf, 2003.

anaesthetic: a drug that blocks a person's sensations of pain

aromatic: having a strong distinctive fragrance

caravan: a group of traders, especially in Africa and Asia, crossing the desert together for safety, usually with a train of camels

dehydrated: preserved by removing natural moisture

dowries: money or property paid to men for marrying women

equator: an imaginary line around Earth that forms a great circle that is the same distance from the North and South Poles

herbs: plants whose leaves, stems, seeds, or roots are used to flavor food, to create medicine, or because they are fragrant

incense: a substance that has a fragrant smell when burned

indigenous: originating in or belonging to a place

malnutrition: a lack of healthy foods

monopoly: to have sole control of a product

mummies: a body that is preserved, dried, and wrapped before being buried

nautical: relating to or involving ships, shipping, navigation, or sailors

navigate: to determine the direction to take on a journey

Phoenicians: ancient sea-faring people who lived to the west of Israel

plague: a serious, sometimes fatal infection transmitted by the bite of an infected flea

resins: solid or semisolid substances obtained from certain plants

scurvy: a disease caused by a lack of vitamin C in the diet

weevils: small beetles that feed on plants and plant products

Age of Exploration 16, 26
archeologists 4
astrolabe 8, 29

cinnamon 4, 6, 7, 14, 15, 23, 24, 27
cloves 4, 5, 6, 10, 24, 27
compass 8

da Gama, Vasco 8, 10, 13, 28
Dutch East India Company 15, 28

Egypt 4, 6, 11

India 6, 7, 8, 10, 11, 14, 15, 28
Indonesia 5, 7, 12, 16, 26
Islam 16, 17, 18, 26

maps 9, 12
Mediterranean 10, 11, 14
monsoon 11

nutmeg 5, 7, 15, 24, 27

pepper 4, 6, 7, 10, 14, 24, 27, 28
Phoenicians 10
Pliny the Elder 22
Portugal 10, 14
Prince Henry the Navigator 28
Prophet Mohammed 16, 17, 18, 28

Queen of Sheba 19

Romans 4, 6, 7, 10, 22
Rome 11

Spain 10, 14, 26
Spice Islands 5, 14, 16, 27

Venice 10, 11, 28

Answers to Quiz on Page 30
1. by 50,000 BC 2. No. It grows on vines. 3. Venice 4. Vasco da Gama
5. 1602 6. Muslim monopoly of the spice trade, to search for knowledge,
to spread Christianity 7. a lack of vitamin C in the diet 8. 20,000
9. the United States 10. Islam